ANCHORED
in
FAITH

CULTURE AND RELIGION ACROSS BORDERS

Dr. ANTONIO R. PAIZ

Sagga Publishing House LLC

Sagga Publishing House, February 2025

Copyright © 2025 by Dr. Antonio R. Paiz

Premium Mass-Market Paperback ISBN: 978-1-964642-03-1

Premium Mass-Market Hardback ISBN: 978-1-964642-14-7

Premium Mass-Market Ebook ISBN: 978-1-964642-04-8

Published in the United States by Sagga Publishing House LLC, Texas.

Printed in the United States of America.

Acknowledgments

First and foremost, I want to give all glory to the Lord for the transformative work He has done in my life and the lives of my family. Through the truth of the Holy Bible, I have come to understand the profound depths of His love, grace, and wisdom. This journey has been enriched by exploring the beliefs, religions, and cultures of others, providing me with a broader perspective and a deeper appreciation of the Word. These experiences have shaped not only my faith but also this work, which stands as a testament to His enduring truth.

I am deeply grateful to the visionary leadership and guidance of the directors at Vision International University in Escondido, California. Their dedication to equipping others for the work of the Lord has been a source of inspiration and encouragement throughout this process.

To my beloved wife, Josephine: your unwavering, godly love and steadfast support have been my rock. Your faith and encouragement have carried me through this journey, and I am forever grateful to you. To my beautiful family: thank you for your love, patience, and belief in me. You are my greatest blessings.

A heartfelt thank you to Sagga Publishing House LLC for bringing this work to life. Your support, professionalism, and commitment to excellence have been invaluable. This book would not have been possible without your partnership.

Finally, to the readers of this work: may it inspire you to seek truth, grow in understanding, and reflect on the profound role of faith in our lives. This book is my offering, born of personal experience, knowledge, and the doctrine of God's Word. To Him be all the glory.

Thank you all.

Preface

Religion has been a cornerstone of human civilization for millennia, shaping cultures, values, and governance. It has offered solace, inspired art, provided moral frameworks, and united communities. Yet, it has also sparked conflicts, justified inequalities, and resisted change. In our modern era, religion finds itself at a crossroads, evolving under the pressure of unprecedented global transformations. This book seeks to explore the multifaceted role of religion in human history and its ongoing metamorphosis in an increasingly secular, pluralistic, and interconnected world.

For much of history, religion was not a matter of choice. It was inherited—woven into the fabric of family, culture, and state. To question it was to risk ostracism or worse. Religions thrived under the patronage of rulers and the implicit acceptance of societies where faith was synonymous with identity. But as modernity unraveled old hierarchies and introduced new freedoms, the certainties of inherited belief systems began to waver. Today, religion is no longer a foregone conclusion; it is a personal decision, shaped by individual experiences, societal norms, and global influences.

This book examines how religion has adapted to these shifting dynamics. It explores the historical roots of major faiths, their core doctrines, and their responses to the challenges of modernity. It delves into the rise of secularism, the fragmentation of religious authority, and the ways in which faith continues to intersect with politics, ethics, and personal identity. From the mystical traditions of Sufism and contemplative practices of Buddhism to the ethical convergences between diverse faiths, we will uncover both the distinctiveness and commonalities of religious traditions.

At its heart, this book is about understanding the fluid nature of belief. It asks: What role does religion play in a world where spiritual choices are no longer confined by geography or tradition? How do faiths evolve when confronted with the demands of modern science, human rights, and global crises? And what can the overlaps and divergences between religions teach us about humanity's shared search for meaning?

Whether you are a believer, skeptic, or seeker, this book invites you to consider the enduring relevance of religion in our rapidly changing world. It does not aim to promote any one belief system, but rather to foster a deeper appreciation for the complexity and richness of human spirituality. By exploring the intersections of history, culture, and faith, we hope to illuminate the ways in which religion continues to shape and be shaped by the human experience.

Welcome to an exploration of Religion, Faith and Culture—an inquiry into how religion has defined us, and how we, in turn, are redefining it.

Contents

ANCHORED

in

FAITH

CULTURE AND RELIGION ACROSS BORDERS

Chapter 1

Faith and Divergence

A Reflection on Religion, Culture, and Truth

On Religion, Culture, and the Pursuit of Truth

I hold a deep respect for Muslims, and I mean this sincerely. However, I believe they are not following the ultimate truth. I offer no apology for this perspective because it is no different from the belief many Muslims hold about Christians—that we, too, have strayed from the right path. According to Islamic theology, Christians rely on a Bible that, in their view, has been corrupted over time. They believe it was once the Word of Allah but argue that the original manuscripts have been lost, leaving only flawed copies.

This critique highlights a significant difference between the first three centuries of Christianity and Islam. Early Christians lived under Roman rule, enduring persecution and hardship, while early Muslims were part of the Khilafah, or Islamic State. Despite the absence of original manuscripts, Christians believe the Bible remains the Word of God. Meanwhile, Muslims are confident the Qur'an remains unchanged from its original form. However, the preservation of a text does not inherently prove its divine origin—just as the ancient Rig Veda, revered in Hindu tradition, is not recognized by Christians or Muslims as the Word of God.

We must seek truth and reject falsehood. As Jesus said, "I am the way, the truth, and the life" (John 14:6).

One of the most significant differences between Islam and Christianity lies in the identity of Jesus. Islam regards Jesus as a prophet—and he is indeed a prophet—but Christianity affirms he is much more: the Savior of humanity. Islam explicitly rejects Jesus as Savior, a fundamental divergence in belief.

Muhammad's Approach to Interfaith Relations

Historically, Muhammad did not compel Jews or Christians to embrace Islam unless they wished to do so voluntarily. The Qur'an strongly advocates against coercion in matters of faith, proclaiming, "There shall be no compulsion in religion" (2:256). Furthermore, it commands Muslims to show respect for Jews and Christians, whom it refers to as "People of the Book" or "People of an Earlier Revelation." Muhammad himself engaged with followers of other faiths in a kindly and respectful manner, provided they were not actively committing evil. He emphasized shared belief in the one God, stating:

"We believe in that which has been bestowed from on high upon us, as well as that which has been bestowed upon you. For our God and your God is one and the same, and it is unto Him that we all surrender ourselves" (Qur'an 29:46).

Today, Islam is the youngest of the three great monotheistic religions, yet it comprises about 1.7 billion followers—roughly one-fifth of the global population. Islam reveres the scriptures of Judaism and Christianity but regards the Qur'an as the final and complete revelation of God.

Religion, Politics, and the Inner Journey

The spiritual quest of religion is deeply personal, an interior journey that transcends politics and external events. Yet, religion often intersects with worldly affairs. Leaders of all faiths—priests, imams, rabbis, and others—have historically grappled with political influence, sometimes relishing it. This intersection has led to interfaith conflicts, persecution of differing beliefs, and struggles for power.

For Christians, Jesus made it clear that his Kingdom "is not of this world" (John 18:36), emphasizing the inward transformation of the believer rather than external dominance. Similarly, in Western secular traditions, religion has often been separated from state affairs to preserve its spiritual integrity.

In contrast, Islam integrates spirituality and governance. The Qur'an gives Muslims a historical mission: to create a just society where all, especially the weak and vulnerable, are treated with respect. This mission ties politics and religion inseparably, as a Muslim's spirituality is intertwined with the pursuit of justice in their community.

Conclusion

As a Christian, there are aspects of Catholicism with which I respectfully disagree. For instance, the concept of purgatory—that souls with minor sins must undergo purification before entering God's presence—does not align with my understanding of Scripture. Similarly, I question practices like indulgent celebrations that conflict with biblical teachings on sobriety and self-control.

"Brethren, ye have been called unto liberty; only use not liberty for an occasion to the flesh, but by love serve one another" (Galatians 5:13).

Ultimately, the pursuit of faith requires humility and a commitment to truth. While our paths and interpretations may differ, our shared longing for the divine unites us in the search for meaning and purpose.

Chapter 2

Christianity

Transformation Through Christ

Defining Christianity: Transformation Through Christ

When Matthew Bell, an Evangelical Christian, engaged in a debate with a Roman Catholic, he offered the following definition of a Christian: "A Christian is an individual whose life has been transformed by the grace of God from a hell-bound sinner to a heaven-bound saint, this being made possible and accomplished by and through the person of Jesus Christ and His efficacious sacrifice."

This definition emphasizes the transformative power of grace and highlights the centrality of Jesus Christ's role in salvation.

Other Evangelicals offer a simpler definition:

"A Christian is a person who has repented of sins and sincerely trusts Jesus as their personal Lord and Savior."

However, some conservative Protestants modify this by omitting the emphasis on repentance. They assert that salvation is entirely dependent on the grace of God and not on any personal effort, including repentance. This perspective underscores the doctrine that salvation is a free gift from God, not earned through human actions.

These definitions share a common theme: they downplay or dismiss the role of sacraments and rituals in salvation. Instead, they emphasize personal repentance and faith in Jesus Christ. By these standards, many Roman Catholics—who view sacraments as a means of receiving God's grace—might not fit the Evangelical definition of a Christian.

The Evangelical Perspective on Salvation

Evangelicals often stress the necessity of being "born again," a phrase drawn from Jesus' conversation with Nicodemus in John 3. According to this view, "true Christians" are those who have experienced a personal spiritual rebirth through the Holy Spirit. As one fundamentalist Christian wrote:

"True Christians are those who are filled with God's Spirit. Anyone not filled with His Spirit is in opposition to God."

This perspective often excludes many who identify as Christians, as it places significant emphasis on a deeply personal, transformative experience with God.

Conservative Protestants frequently refer to an "invisible church"—a body of true believers united by their faith in Jesus Christ, regardless of denominational differences. They believe this invisible church exists amidst the imperfections and sins of humanity.

The Inward Need for Christ

Evangelical theology often emphasizes humanity's inherent emptiness—a void that can only be filled by a relationship with God through Jesus Christ. People may attempt to fill this void with material possessions, pleasures, or worldly pursuits, but these efforts lead to temporary satisfaction at best. Only Christ can provide lasting fulfillment:

"The eyes of the Lord are on those who fear Him, on those who hope for His lovingkindness, to deliver their soul from death and to keep them alive in famine" (Psalm 34:18-21).

The Apostle Paul further explained this transformation in 2 Corinthians 5:17:

"Therefore, if anyone is in Christ, he is a new creature; old things have passed away; behold, all things have become new."

This newness in Christ is not merely external but signifies a complete inner renewal—a departure from the old, sinful nature and an embrace of a life aligned with God's will.

Born Again: A New Life in Christ

The Book of Hebrews admonishes believers to grow in holiness and spiritual maturity, relying on the intercession of Christ as their High Priest. Jesus, who understands human struggles, stands as an advocate for those who seek Him:

"For we have not a high priest which cannot be touched with the feeling of our infirmities; but was in all points tempted like as we are, yet without sin" (Hebrews 4:15).

This provision assures believers that they can overcome trials and spiritual defeats by drawing upon the mercy and grace of Jesus Christ.

Revelation 12:11 further highlights the victory of the saints:

"They overcame [the accuser] by the blood of the Lamb and the word of their testimony."

This victory is not limited to martyrs but extends to all born-again believers who live out their faith daily.

The Importance of Faith and Confession

To experience the fullness of salvation, believers must recognize and confess their faith in Jesus Christ:

"If you confess with your mouth, 'Jesus is Lord,' and believe in your heart that God raised Him from the dead, you will be saved" (Romans 10:9).

Faith must be active, not passive. As James wrote, "Faith without works is dead" (James 2:17). This faith grows stronger through personal testimonies and continual confession of God's promises.

Paul's exhortation to the Ephesians underscores the call to transformation:

"Put off your old self, which is being corrupted by its deceitful desires; to be made new in the attitude of your minds; and to put on the new self, created to be like God in true righteousness and holiness" (Ephesians 4:22-24)

Conclusion

A true Christian life is one of transformation—leaving behind sin and embracing a new identity in Christ. This change is not about ritual or external observance but about a deep, personal relationship with Jesus. Evangelicals emphasize that salvation is a free gift, offered through the grace of God and accessed by faith. This grace empowers believers to live victorious, purposeful lives, reflecting the love and truth of Christ to the world.

Chapter 3

Ancient Egyptian Beliefs
Legacy of Eternity

Ancient Egyptian Religion: A Complex Legacy

Despite the familiarity of its images and symbols today, ancient Egyptian religion remains conceptually distant from modern understanding. Its pluralities—regional theologies, cosmogonies, a pantheon of merging gods, and varying myths—often appear contradictory when viewed retrospectively. Even foundational elements, such as the divinity of the pharaoh and the nature of the afterlife, remain subjects of debate among scholars.

This deeply conservative religious tradition sought to preserve the status quo in every aspect of life. Its heroes and historical narratives were shaped into archetypal patterns that upheld an ideal vision of eternal, static perfection. This vision of the afterlife—a harmonious existence beyond the chaos of earthly life—has fascinated and provoked the imagination of observers for centuries.

Early Egyptian Religion: Kingship and Theology

The early period of Egyptian religion, around 3000 BCE, marked the unification of Upper and Lower Egypt under the first dynasty. Alongside the emergence of hieroglyphic writing and a distinctive iconographic style, kingship became a central aspect of Egyptian theology.

The Narmer Palette, a key artifact from this period, depicts the king wearing the crowns of both Upper and Lower Egypt, symbolizing unification. Early kings aligned themselves with the god Horus, and later dynasties incorporated Seth, resulting in the "Horus and Seth" title for the king. This association elevated the king to a superhuman status, a tradition that endured as a powerful political tool.

The Old Kingdom (c. 2686–2181 BCE) saw the construction of the great pyramids and complex funerary texts. These inscriptions, along with early theological writings, provide insights into Egyptian beliefs about the afterlife, divine order, and the role of the king.

Creation Myths and Cosmogony

Egyptian creation myths varied by region but often shared common themes. At Hermopolis, for example, the creation of the world began with the emergence of an egg from a primordial watery chaos. In Heliopolis, a primordial hill was believed to mark the starting point of creation. The creator god Atum was said to have emerged from this chaos, later evolving into more complex myths where gods like Ptah superseded Atum through more refined theological interpretations.

These myths reflect a profound attempt to understand existence and the divine order, blending symbolic acts such as the "expectoration" of the creator god with more philosophical traditions of divine conception and articulation.

Religious Practices and Popular Piety

Egyptian temples were considered the "houses" of gods, accessible only to ritually clean priests. These priests cared for the deities' images, performed offerings, and organized festivals, which often included elaborate processions and rituals immortalized in wall paintings.

For ordinary Egyptians, religious practice was often intertwined with daily life. Amulets, scarabs, and figurines were used for protection and healing, while magic, considered a divine gift, played a significant role in personal and communal rituals. Spells recorded on papyrus or pottery invoked the aid of gods, who were sometimes believed to be magically coerced to act on behalf of their devotees.

Festivals, such as the carrying of a god's ceremonial boat, were occasions of music, dance, and public celebration. Osiris, the god of rebirth and the judge of the dead, held a prominent place in popular piety. His burial site at Abydos became a major pilgrimage center, attracting votive offerings and prayers from people across Egypt.

The Afterlife and Mummification

Belief in life after death emerged early in Egyptian culture, as evidenced by prehistoric burial practices. The dead were interred facing west, accompanied by grave goods for the afterlife. As tomb construction replaced simple graves, the practice of mummification developed to preserve the body for eternity.

The elaborate care given to the dead reflected the Egyptians' belief that physical preservation was essential for the survival of the spirit. Food, clothing, and other goods were buried alongside the deceased to ensure their comfort in the afterlife. For the Egyptians, this continuation of life was a central focus of their religious worldview.

Conclusion

While the Egyptians' intricate religious system and their focus on the afterlife offer valuable insights into their worldview, their beliefs stand in stark contrast to those of Christianity. Jesus Christ proclaimed:

"I am the resurrection, and the life: he that believeth in me, though he were dead, yet shall he live" (John 11:25).

As a Christian, I believe in life after death, but not through the preservation of a physical body or adherence to complex rituals. Eternal life is found through faith in Jesus Christ, who offers salvation and renewal.

The Egyptian focus on mummification, their pantheon of gods, and their conception of the afterlife, while fascinating, do not align with the truth revealed in Christ. Their practices and beliefs, though rich in cultural significance, fall short of the ultimate hope and assurance found in the Gospel.

Chapter 4

Ancient Irish Beliefs

From Superstition to Spiritual Fulfillment

Ancient Irish Superstitions and Spiritual Beliefs

The superstitions of a people often reflect the remnants of their ancient faiths. As one scholar notes, "much of the religion of the lower orders, which we regard as essentially divine, is ancient heathenism refined with Christian symbols." While elements of these beliefs persist, they often represent the enduring legacy of pre-Christian traditions.

Dreams, Miracles, and Transformations

Dreams held significant spiritual importance in ancient Ireland. St. Patrick's *Confession* references dreams, while other signs, such as the flight of birds, movements of beasts, and formations of clouds, were interpreted as omens. Prodigies and miracles were often reported but typically witnessed only by select individuals.

Stories of transformations, particularly into animals, reflect a possible connection to totemism. Druids, according to tradition, could change men into animals or trees. Similarly, witchcraft was believed to grant individuals the power to manipulate natural laws, consciously or unconsciously. Examples include hypnotizing enemies to see rocks as armed soldiers and tying cursed knots in strings to cause harm—practices that could be undone by unraveling the knots. Other fantastical traditions include:

- **Fairy Gifts**: A thimble that transformed into a boat.

- **Shapeshifting**: Adepts turning into vultures, swans, or wolves.

- **Magical Creatures**: A large white cat claiming to be a 300-year-old woman.

While these beliefs may appear nonsensical, they reflect the imaginative and deeply spiritual worldview of the Irish people.

Lamentations and Death Rituals

Irish mourning customs, such as *keening*, have roots in pre-Christian traditions. Professional mourners were hired to perform wailing laments, creating an eerie atmosphere that symbolized the passage of the deceased into another realm.

Some lamentations, however, displayed profound emotional depth and poetic beauty. For instance:

"My sunshine you were. I loved you better than the sun itself; and when I see the sun going down in the west, I think of my boy, and my black night of sorrow. Like the rising sun, he had a red glow on his cheek. He was as bright as the sun at mid-day; but a dark storm came on, and my sunshine was lost to me forever."

While such expressions often lacked Christian origins, they resonated with the universal human experience of grief and loss.

Belief in Spirits and Ghosts

The Irish imagination has long been captivated by spirits, ghosts, and supernatural beings. Stories of ghosts and spiritual entities were common, with many believing in invisible intermediaries (*diamones*) who existed between God and humanity. These spirits were thought to understand human thoughts and could be summoned through local rituals.

Ghost stories, often passed down orally, were not unique to Ireland. Across cultures and centuries, such tales reflected deep-seated fears and curiosities about the unseen world. Figures like Martin Luther and John Wesley acknowledged the existence of spirits, lending credence to these beliefs in their time.

Spiritual Protection in Faith

While ancient Irish superstitions reflect a search for security and protection, the Bible offers a contrasting perspective on divine refuge. Moses, in his prayer, writes:

"I will say of the Lord, He is my refuge and my fortress: my God; in him will I trust. Surely he shall deliver thee from the snare of the fowler, and from the noisome pestilence." (Psalm 91:2-3)

The psalmist emphasizes that God's truth serves as a shield, offering protection from the dangers of both night and day:

"Thou shalt not be afraid for the terror by night; nor for the arrow that flieth by day; nor for the pestilence that walketh in darkness; nor for the destruction that wasteth at noonday." (Psalm 91:5-6)

In this view, ultimate security lies in faith in God, not in superstitions or magical rituals.

Christian Faith vs. Superstitious Beliefs

The persistence of superstitions, both in ancient Ireland and today, reflects humanity's enduring struggle to understand the spiritual world. While these beliefs often stemmed from genuine attempts to navigate life's uncertainties, they ultimately fall short of the truth found in Jesus Christ.

As the Apostle Paul reminds us, true spiritual freedom and protection come through Christ alone. The ancient superstitions, like modern-day misconceptions, serve as a reminder of the need for a faith grounded in God's Word.

"If God be for us, who can be against us?" (Romans 8:31)

By turning to Christ, believers find not only protection but also a transformative relationship with the Creator, offering hope and peace that no superstition can provide.

Conclusion

The ancient superstitions of Ireland, while fascinating, reflect a spiritual yearning that is ultimately fulfilled in the gospel. As imaginative as these beliefs were, they point to humanity's universal need for security, guidance, and understanding. In Christ, this need finds its ultimate resolution, offering a refuge that transcends fear and superstition.

Chapter 5

Buddhism Across Cultures
Adaptation, Practice, and Perception in the West

Initial Impressions

R eading about the history and beliefs of Buddhism, I did not feel the excitement that typically accompanies the discovery of a timeless and culturally enriching perspective on the Buddha-dharma. Instead, I was troubled by a growing trend to distort and dilute Buddhist teachings, seemingly to make meditation practices more palatable and marketable in today's spiritual marketplace.

Buddhism's Journey: Westward and Eastward

Buddhist pilgrims carried their ideas and practices far from India. Historical records, such as Asokan edicts, document dharma envoys sent to Syria, Egypt, and Macedonia. Some speculate that Buddhist monks may have reached the Mediterranean and influenced Greek philosophy or early Christianity, but concrete evidence is lacking.

The eastward spread of Buddhism is well-documented, from its arrival in China by the first century C.E. to Japan via Korea by the twelfth century. Intriguingly, some scholars propose that Buddhist monks may have ventured as far as Alaska and Mexico, potentially influencing Huichol Indian culture and DNA—a claim that, if true, predates Columbus by a millennium.

Buddhism Begins with a Man

Buddhism's roots trace back to a man whose teachings ignited India and drew the reverence of kings. People approached him with profound questions—not "Who are you?" concerning lineage, but "What are you? What order of being do you represent?" Such inquiries are rare in history and have been directed at only two figures: Jesus and the Buddha. The Buddha's response shaped the core identity of his teachings, resonating across centuries.

The Wheel of Dharma and Messiah Parallels

Buddhist societies recognize two "world-moving wheels": the wheel of political power (*anachakra*) and the wheel of dharma. The Buddha's followers titled him *Chakravartin*, or "wheel turner," for setting the dharma in motion to awaken and benefit all beings. This dual meaning finds parallels in the messianic stories of other traditions, including Christianity.

Buddhism in North America

The first style of Asian Buddhism to take root in North America was Zen, and it remains the most prominent. While comprehensive data on Buddhist affiliations in the West is scarce, many groups focusing on meditation reflect the influence of the "New Buddhism," which adapts traditional practices for modern contexts.

A Universal Perspective on Suffering

Romanticizing one culture while condemning another obscures the universal nature of suffering. For example, child abuse and neglect are not unique to North America. Ancient India, during the Buddha's time, faced its own challenges. The Four Noble Truths, foundational to all Buddhist traditions, emphasize this universality, offering a framework for spiritual practice that transcends cultural boundaries.

Korean and Japanese Zen: A Cultural Comparison

Japanese immigrants were instrumental in bringing Zen to North America, but their influence was minimal in Great Britain, where Zen is less common. Korean Buddhism, represented by the Chogye Order, combines meditation, academic sutra study, and Pure Land practices. Compared to the formality of Japanese Zen, Korean Zen in the West feels more casual, with distinct differences in terminology, rituals, and aesthetics.

The Evolution of Zen in the West

Zen Buddhism has adapted significantly in the West. Without an overarching hierarchy, individual teachers and groups shape their own approaches. Authentic Zen is not defined by rigid doctrines but by its connection to the tradition passed through generations. Western Zen centers often emphasize discipline and structure, but their formality may feel unfamiliar to casual visitors.

Ritual as Practice

Unlike theistic religions that aim to glorify a deity, Zen rituals, such as chanting and bowing, are not obligations to a divine figure. Instead, they are valued for their meditative quality. The meticulous performance of rituals is seen as an integral part of spiritual practice, fostering mindfulness and presence.

Conclusion

Buddhism's journey from ancient India to its modern Western adaptations highlights its remarkable resilience and adaptability. However, the tension between preserving the integrity of its teachings and meeting contemporary demands raises important questions about the future of this timeless tradition in a rapidly changing world.

Chapter 6

A Creole Religion in Jamaica

The Origins of Revival

The Evolution of Jamaican Religion

J amaican religion evolved as a complex response to historical, social, and cultural factors. The oppressive conditions of slavery, the diverse composition of the enslaved population, economic deprivation, natural disasters, and systemic racial stratification profoundly shaped its development. Over time, religion in Jamaica became a critical force in the creation of a Creole culture, fusing African and European traditions and mitigating cultural dissonance.

Throughout Jamaica's history, religious expressions have included a vibrant array of cults, sects, movements, prophets, healers, and sorcerers. Each phase of cultural evolution in Jamaica has been marked by religious innovations, with syncretic movements playing a central role in transforming and adapting spiritual practices to the island's unique social landscape.

Religious Diversity and Christian Influence

Jamaica is an intensely religious society, predominantly Christian with a strong emphasis on Protestant fundamentalism. Its religious practices include congregational, millenarian, salvationist, evangelical, and charismatic orientations. Over the decades, the growth of fundamentalist, evangelical, and Pentecostal movements has been notable, beginning with the Adventist Church and expanding to various forms of the Church of God, especially in parishes like Clarendon. While some sects maintain affiliations with American denominations, many have taken on distinctly Jamaican identities and are largely under local control.

Revival Ideology

Revivalist traditions in Jamaica often emphasize Old Testament teachings, depicting God as both protective and punitive. Adherents value humility, self-sacrifice, mutual support, and spiritual contentment, viewing themselves as "the meek and the lowly." In recent years, a shift toward New Testament themes has brought greater emphasis on moral self-improvement, spiritual rebirth, and the pursuit of love, joy, and holiness. Revivalists also believe in the active presence of angels, often regarded as intermediaries between God and humanity. These angels provide protection and warnings through dreams, interpreted by cult leaders.

Ritual practices such as the "Nine-Night" wake or "setup" aim to pacify spirits of the deceased, followed by ceremonies like the Tambling ritual and annual memorial services. Revivalist worship is vibrant and communal, combining traditional hymns, rhythmic choruses, and ecstatic dancing accompanied by tambourines and goat-skin drums. Participants often enter trance states or exhibit manifestations of the Holy Spirit, including speaking in tongues and "shouting" dances.

Combating Destruction: Illness and Misfortune

Central to Revivalist beliefs is the concept of "destruction," which encompasses illness, misfortune, and spiritual attacks attributed to supernatural forces such as duppies (ghosts) and demons. Rituals to combat destruction include exorcisms, protective charms, and healing services. Some Revivalists operate balm yards, where spiritual healing is practiced full-time, blending African traditions with Christian elements.

Obeah and African Traditions

Obeah, an indigenous Jamaican practice rooted in African traditions, remains an influential system for addressing supernatural problems. Obeah practitioners are believed to wield spiritual power to capture duppies, cast spells, and offer protective charms. Historically, obeah men used items like feathers, bones, and grave dirt in rituals to harm or protect individuals. Although many view these practices as malevolent, others seek out obeah practitioners for assistance in personal and legal matters.

African Roots and Syncretism

The foundation of Jamaican religious practices lies in the African spiritual systems brought to the island by enslaved peoples. These systems emphasized a supreme creator deity, intermediary spirits, ancestor worship, and elaborate rituals involving singing, drumming, and ceremonial possession. Despite the devastating effects of slavery, which disrupted traditional practices, African religious elements persisted and adapted through cultural synthesis.

This syncretism became evident as slaves incorporated Christian symbols, figures, and rituals into African practices. The Bible, the cross, and baptism were repurposed for spiritual protection, while Christian figures such as angels and John the Baptist were assimilated into the African pantheon. Sin and sorcery became equated, and ceremonial possession was reinterpreted as a manifestation of the Holy Spirit.

Conclusion

Throughout Jamaican history, religious revivals have played a critical role in renewing and restoring faith. These "waves" or "movements" reflect God's ongoing efforts to remind humanity of His Word. Each revival has been grounded in scriptural truths, underscoring the enduring relevance of the Bible as a source of spiritual guidance.

Jamaica's religious landscape, marked by its rich blend of African and European influences, continues to evolve. Its enduring traditions testify to the resilience and creativity of its people, who have transformed faith into a powerful tool for navigating the complexities of history, culture, and identity.

Chapter 7

Modern Hinduism
Tradition, Reform, and Global Influence

The Emergence of Modern Hinduism

The concept of "modern Hinduism" resists a simplistic division into "pre-modern" and "modern" periods. Hinduism's origins and histories are too varied to warrant such rigid periodization. What is often referred to as "modern Hinduism" represents sporadic and episodic movements that arose in response to European colonial powers' presence in India from the early 19th century onward.

Mainstream Hindu traditions—Vaishnavism, Shaivism, Shaktism, and various smaller *sampradayas*—continue to command the allegiance of the majority of Hindus. While these traditions have adapted to changing circumstances over time, they cannot be globally categorized as "pre-modern."

The Role of Reform Movements

The 19th and 20th centuries saw a series of Hindu reform movements that significantly influenced Hinduism. Interestingly, these movements did not transform Hinduism by amassing large followings. Many had relatively small memberships, and some disappeared entirely. Their primary impact lay in stimulating traditional Hinduism to adapt and evolve.

These movements also played a pivotal role in bringing Hinduism to the West, reversing the trajectory of Christian missions, which had long established themselves in India. As a result, Hindu ideas began to find a place in the spiritual landscape of the Western world, challenging long-held assumptions about Western religion's sufficiency in meeting spiritual needs.

Early Western Contact with Hinduism

Western contact with India began with Vasco da Gama's historic voyage around the Cape of Good Hope in 1498. Over the subsequent centuries, European powers, including the Portuguese, Dutch, Danes, English, and French, established trading posts and colonies in India. Alongside merchants and soldiers came Christian missionaries, who encountered Hinduism as a complex and deeply ingrained religious tradition.

To their surprise, missionaries also discovered an ancient group of Indian Christians who were unaware of the Pope's authority. While many missionaries were hostile toward Hinduism, others provided valuable documentation about India's religions. However, early scholars faced significant challenges in studying Hinduism. The Brahmins, protective of their sacred knowledge, were reluctant to teach Sanskrit or share their scriptures. By this period, Hinduism had become inward-looking, defensive, and secretive, compounding the difficulty of understanding its traditions.

The Hindu Renaissance

The decline of the Mughal Empire and the rise of European colonial powers coincided with Hindu resistance to Westernization and Christianization. This period, often referred to as the "Hindu Renaissance," marked a restoration and reinterpretation of Indian traditions against the backdrop of Western dominance.

Some traditional Hindus responded defensively, writing apologetic tracts in Sanskrit to counter foreign influences. Others recognized the need for change to preserve India's identity and soul in a rapidly modernizing world. These early reformers faced significant risks:

1. **Contact with Foreigners:** They had to defy Hindu rules prohibiting interactions with *mlecchas* (impure foreigners).

2. **Critical Analysis:** They critically examined their own traditions instead of passively submitting to the decisions of pundits.

3. **Abandoning Sacred Customs:** They had to relinquish aspects of the sacred order of life to engage meaningfully with the modern world.

One of the earliest and most influential reformers serves as a notable example of this transformative period.

The Spread of Hinduism to the West

In recent decades, Hindu religious movements have proliferated in the West. These movements, either imported from India or initiated locally, are so diverse that it is difficult to provide a comprehensive account or assessment.

An Indian writer humorously remarked that the ordination (*abhisheka*) of a modern Hindu Swami now includes a jet trip to America. These movements vary significantly in focus and scope. Some are extensions of Indian *sampradayas* (religious traditions) aimed at preserving their heritage, while others are specifically tailored to Western audiences.

Despite their diversity, these movements share a common thread: a universalist vision that transcends cultural and geographical boundaries. This universality has allowed Hindu ideas to resonate in the spiritually curious and eclectic environment of the contemporary West.

Conclusion

The history of modern Hinduism is a story of adaptation and exchange, shaped by colonial encounters, reform movements, and global expansion. While traditional Hinduism has retained its core practices and beliefs, it has also evolved in response to new challenges and opportunities.

In the West, Hinduism has sparked both interest and alarm, seen by some as a valuable spiritual alternative and by others as incompatible with traditional Western religions and scientific rationalism. Nevertheless, its universalist claims and emphasis on spiritual exploration continue to attract diverse audiences, ensuring its relevance in an increasingly interconnected world.

Chapter 8

Jehova's Witnesses
The Socialization of Children

One of the clearest examples of Jehovah's Witnesses' opposition to modern societal norms is their approach to socializing second and subsequent generations within their faith. Many Witness parents introduce their children to Watch Tower teachings from an early age, aiming to secure baptism and lifelong commitment. Bringing young children to Kingdom Hall meetings serves two essential purposes: recruiting new members to sustain the faith and protecting the most impressionable members from perceived worldly corruption.

The Watch Tower Society circulates millions of tracts aimed at young people, addressing topics such as morality, welfare, and personal happiness. Simultaneously, the organization provides parents with extensive guidance on raising children in a world often seen as hostile to their beliefs. This includes materials on managing rebellious children, reflecting the Society's broader focus on shaping both childhood and parenting within its framework.

Socialization and Parenting Strategies

Jehovah's Witnesses invest significant time and effort in educating their children according to Watch Tower principles. From an early age—sometimes as soon as they can walk—children are immersed in the spiritual activities of the Society.

For a movement that prioritizes insularity and often struggles to attract new members, children are viewed as a crucial resource for its survival.

While the hope of every Witness parent is that their children will remain loyal to the faith, approaches to parenting vary significantly. Differences manifest in areas such as discipline enforcement, the extent of association with non-Witness peers, and the level of participation in Watch Tower activities. Mixed marriages, in particular, often lead to divergent parenting practices.

Parents are encouraged to uphold authority and instill respect, as emphasized in Watch Tower literature. For example, Proverbs 30:17 and Proverbs 23:22 are often cited to reinforce the idea that children must honor their parents, even if family life is imperfect. This conservative appeal to authority aligns with a broader reluctance within the faith to tolerate dissent or questioning, especially from younger members.

Children's Participation in Witness Activities

Children's involvement in Kingdom Hall and book study meetings begins at a young age, with even four- and five-year-olds volunteering answers during discussions. As they grow older, their participation increases, culminating in role-playing sessions to prepare for door-to-door evangelism. Children often undertake this ministry alongside close relatives, such as parents or siblings, further reinforcing family-based socialization.

The Society relies heavily on familial bonds to ensure children are effectively integrated into its belief system. Studying Watch Tower tracts and participating in Kingdom Hall activities become central to family life. Discipline is a critical component, with parents acting as enforcers of the Society's rules. While some parents adopt a strict approach, including verbal or physical reprimands, others are more lenient, highlighting variability within the community.

Control and the Illusion of Choice

Jehovah's Witnesses argue that they exercise free choice within the confines of their faith. However, the selection is strictly limited, creating an illusion of autonomy. This method of control is effective because it fosters a sense of agency while restricting options. Witnesses trust the Governing Body implicitly, viewing its guidance as divinely inspired. This trust leads to unquestioning obedience, with members willing to follow directives without hesitation.

Critics argue that this dynamic amounts to mind control. The Governing Body's centralized authority influences millions of adherents, shaping their decisions and beliefs. Any dissent or questioning of the need for such an organization is strongly discouraged, further consolidating its control.

Conclusion

Jehovah's Witnesses' approach to socialization and parenting reflects their broader efforts to preserve their faith in a changing world. By instilling Watch Tower principles from an early age and fostering strict adherence to its teachings, the Society seeks to protect its members and maintain its identity. However, this insular approach also raises questions about individual autonomy and the balance between faith and freedom. As the Witnesses continue to navigate modern challenges, their practices and structures remain a subject of scrutiny and debate.

Chapter 9

John Calvin's Geneva
Worship, Theology, and Governance Redefined

Worship, Theology, and Governance in Geneva

John Calvin's Reformed tradition shared many convictions with Roman Catholics, Lutherans, Anabaptists, and other Protestants. However, where Martin Luther emphasized justification by grace and faith alone, Calvin and his followers focused on the glory of God as central to all aspects of life.

In his seminal work, *Institutes of the Christian Religion*, Calvin articulated his vision:

"We are consecrated and dedicated to God in order that we may thereafter think, speak, meditate, and do nothing except to his glory... We are God's: let us therefore live for him and die for him. We are God's: let his wisdom and will therefore rule all our actions. We are God's: let all the parts of our life accordingly strive toward him as our only lawful goal."

This biblical vision of a God who governs all of life shaped Reformed worship, theology, governance, and the Christian life.

Worship in the Reformed Tradition

For Calvin and the Reformed tradition, worship was the Christian's highest service to God, inspired and supported by the Holy Spirit. Worship included the preaching and hearing of the Word and the sacraments instituted by Jesus Christ.

Calvin's Approach to Worship

In Geneva, Calvin laid out his vision for worship:

1. Biblical Orientation: Worship was grounded in Scripture, with theological integrity and simplicity.

2. Edification of the Community: Worship aimed to build up the Christian community.

3. Written and Spontaneous Prayers: Calvin incorporated both structured and free prayer forms.

Calvin's liturgical order began with Psalm 124:8:

"Our help is in the name of the LORD, who made heaven and earth."

The first part of the service focused on the preaching of the Word, invigorated by the accessibility of the Bible in the vernacular rather than Latin.

Sacraments in Reformed Worship

The Reformed tradition retained only Baptism and the Lord's Supper from the medieval sacramental system:

- Baptism: Administered through sprinkling, including to infants of believing parents.

- The Lord's Supper: Calvin taught that Christ was spiritually present in the sacrament, rejecting the doctrine of transubstantiation. He desired weekly communion but compromised with Geneva's civil authorities, scheduling services across the city to ensure the sacrament was observed every Lord's Day.

Music in Worship

The Reformed tradition became known for its Psalm singing, as Psalms were considered biblically orthodox. Calvin supported congregational singing, even defending Louis Bourgeois, the city's music director, when he was jailed for altering hymn tunes. Calvin reassured magistrates that these changes aimed to enhance worship, though the tunes were derisively nicknamed "Geneva jigs."

Liturgy of the Word and the Upper Room

In 1542, Calvin formalized a liturgy that structured morning worship into two parts:

The Liturgy of the Word

1. Scripture Sentence: Psalm 124:8

2. Confession of Sins and Prayer for Pardon

3. Metrical Psalm

4. Collect for Illumination

5. Lection

6. Sermon

The Liturgy of the Upper Room

1. Collection of Alms

2. Intercessions and the Lord's Prayer (paraphrased)

3. Preparation of Elements (sung with the Apostles' Creed)

4. Words of Institution

5. Exhortation

6. Consecration Prayer

7. Fraction, Delivery, and Communion (accompanied by Psalms or Scripture)

8. Post-Communion Collect

9. Aaronic Blessing

Reformed Theology

Calvin's theology, most extensively expressed in his *Institutes*, emphasized:

1. Scriptural Authority: Theology was based solely on Scripture.

2. Creeds and Trinitarian Doctrine: The Reformed accepted the ancient creeds, including the Apostles' Creed, which was recited in worship.

3. The Nature of God: God could only be known as Creator and Redeemer, as revealed through the Holy Spirit's testimony in the heart.

4. Human Nature: Humans, created in God's image, were called to stewardship of creation, which awaited ultimate redemption (Romans 8:22).

The Church in Reformed Theology

The Reformed view of the church was both spiritual and practical:

1. A Community of Faith: Christians belonged to a "communion of saints," encompassing the living and the dead, known only to God.

2. The Visible and Invisible Church: The visible church served as a primary structure of grace, while the invisible church represented the true body of Christ, known only to God.

3. Jesus Christ as Head: The Reformed rejected the pope's authority, viewing Christ as the sole head of the church.

Church Governance

Governance in the Christian community was an expression of belief. Calvin articulated these ideas in his *Ecclesiastical Ordinances* (1541) and the *Institutes*. Other Reformed leaders expanded on these principles in confessional documents and statements about church government.

The Reformed tradition emphasized shared governance, often employing presbyterian structures where leadership was distributed among elders. This system contrasted sharply with hierarchical models, such as those in the Roman Catholic Church.

Conclusion

John Calvin's Reformed tradition profoundly shaped worship, theology, and church governance in Geneva and beyond. His emphasis on the glory of God, scriptural authority, and the centrality of Christ inspired a movement that redefined Christian life and thought. While rooted in tradition, the Reformed faith sought to renew the church and align all aspects of life with God's will, leaving an enduring legacy in the global Christian community.

Chapter 10

Judaism

A Covenant of Faith, Ethics, and Enduring Legacy

Judaism: A Small Nation with a Monumental Legacy

There are approximately fifteen million Jews in the world today, with six million living in the United States and three million in Israel. This number, referring to individuals of Jewish descent, not all of whom practice the religion, is remarkably small given the profound influence Judaism has exerted on global history and culture.

One of history's great ironies is that three of the world's major religions—Judaism, Christianity, and Islam—trace their origins to the beliefs of a seemingly insignificant people. While ancient empires such as Egypt, Assyria, Babylonia, Persia, and Rome rose and fell, the Jewish nation, small and often marginalized, persisted. Outsiders regarded the Jews as eccentric and backward, devoted to peculiar practices and a single irritable deity. Yet, as these great empires crumbled, Judaism profoundly shaped the religious, moral, and cultural foundations of millions of people. Believers see this as evidence of divine providence.

A Religion Marked by Persecution

Despite its influence, Judaism has faced relentless persecution, especially at the hands of Christianity, a religion that emerged from its teachings. A key reason for this lies in Judaism's dual identity as both a religious and racial phenomenon. A Jew is defined as anyone born to Jewish parents or anyone who professes the Jewish faith. Unlike Christianity and Islam, Judaism has rarely sought converts, and most Jews are born into their faith. This makes it difficult for outsiders to adopt Judaism, as conversion requires embracing an entire way of life that encompasses faith, customs, and community.

This exclusivity has often positioned Jews as outsiders, leading to centuries of shunning and persecution. Additionally, the Jewish belief in being God's "chosen people," tasked with bringing the world to His service, has at times been misinterpreted as national self-centeredness, further fueling anti-Semitism.

Core Beliefs and Teachings

Judaism is strictly monotheistic. The Shema, a declaration of faith from Deuteronomy 6:4, encapsulates this belief:

"Hear, O Israel: The Lord our God, the Lord is One."

This verse is central to Jewish worship and is recited daily by devout Jews. It is also spoken during one's final moments, reinforcing the unwavering commitment to God's singularity. Consequently, Judaism rejects the Christian doctrines of the Trinity and the divinity of Christ, viewing them as deviations from true monotheism.

The Hebrew Bible, or the Old Testament as Christians call it, is revered as the Word of God. The Torah, comprising the first five books attributed to Moses, holds particular significance. It narrates the history of the world, the formation of Israel as a nation, and the laws given to Moses, including the Ten Commandments and numerous moral, ritual, and dietary laws. These laws reflect a time when morality, ritual, and custom were inseparable.

Ethical Emphasis in Judaism

While Jewish law encompasses a wide range of prescriptions, from dietary restrictions to rituals for purification, the religion emphasizes ethics above all. Prophets and teachers have repeatedly stressed that moral behavior and genuine repentance outweigh strict adherence to ritual. The essential moral teachings of Judaism, such as the Ten Commandments, have become the foundation of the Western ethical framework.

Historical Origins

The origins of Judaism are rooted in the stories of the Hebrew Bible. According to Deuteronomy 26, the history of the Jewish people begins with nomadic Semitic tribes who settled in Egypt. Over time, they grew in number and were enslaved by the Egyptians. Their liberation, led by Moses, forms a central narrative in Jewish tradition.

Traditions trace the Jewish lineage back to Jacob, also known as Israel, who personifies the nation. Jacob's twelve sons are said to have founded the twelve tribes of Israel. Further back, Jacob is linked to Abraham, who migrated from Ur in Mesopotamia to Canaan at God's command. This migration established Canaan as the God-given homeland for Abraham's descendants and introduced circumcision as a sign of the covenant.

The Role of Moses

The first indisputably historical figure in Jewish tradition is Moses, the leader of the Exodus. While scholars debate the exact timeline, one theory places Moses in Egypt around 1250 BCE during the reign of Pharaoh Ramses II, while another suggests an earlier date during Pharaoh Thutmose III.

Moses' story begins with his escape to the desert after killing an Egyptian who was mistreating a Hebrew. In the wilderness, he encountered God in a burning bush and received his divine mission: to lead the Israelites out of Egypt. When Moses asked for God's name, the reply was, "I am who I am," a phrase often rendered as Yahweh, emphasizing God's eternal and self-existent nature.

The Exodus story recounts God's dramatic deliverance of the Israelites, including the parting of the Red Sea and the drowning of Pharaoh's pursuing army. Moses then led the people to Mount Sinai, where he received the Ten Commandments and established the covenant between God and Israel.

A Religion of Covenant and Continuity

Judaism is founded on the covenant, an agreement by which God commits Himself to Israel as His chosen people. This relationship is marked by a deep sense of divine justice, moral obligation, and historical continuity.

The journey of the Jewish people—from their early nomadic origins to their role as a significant religious and cultural force—offers profound insights into the resilience of faith and the enduring power of ethical monotheism.

Conclusion

As a Christian, I respect the profound legacy of Judaism and its foundational role in shaping the moral and spiritual fabric of the world. However, I believe that ultimate salvation and eternal life are found in Jesus Christ, who said:

"I am the resurrection and the life. The one who believes in me will live, even though they die" (John 11:25).

While Judaism has contributed immeasurably to humanity's spiritual heritage, its emphasis on the law and rituals contrasts with the grace and redemption offered through Christ.

Chapter 11

Lutheranism

Reformation Legacy and the Pursuit of Truth

Lutheranism: The Purest Form of Protestantism?

Lutheranism is often regarded as the purest form of Protestantism. The term "Protestant" itself was coined by Martin Luther, who referred to himself as *Protestor Fidei*, meaning "A Witness to the Faith." Ironically, Lutheranism retains many traditional Catholic elements, including liturgy and some theological practices, making it closer to Roman Catholicism than many other Protestant traditions. Despite lacking an episcopate in the apostolic succession, Lutheranism shares enough characteristics with other historic branches of Christianity—Eastern Orthodox, Roman Catholic, and Anglican Churches—that it could be considered a "catholic" (universal) church.

The term "Lutheran" was originally used pejoratively by the enemies of the movement. Luther himself disliked it, preferring the name "Evangelical Church of the Augsburg Confession." Over time, however, his followers embraced the term, transforming it into a badge of honor.

Martin Luther: Father of Protestantism

Martin Luther is widely recognized as the father of Protestantism. While he was not the first to challenge the authority of the Roman Catholic Church, he was instrumental in crystallizing the growing discontent into what became known as the Protestant Reformation.

Born in Eisleben, Germany, Luther initially pursued a career in law, completing his master's degree before entering law school in 1505. However, a profound religious experience prompted him to abandon his legal studies and join a monastery in Erfurt. Ordained as a priest in 1507, he was later appointed to teach theology at the University of Wittenberg in Saxony.

A trip to Rome profoundly impacted Luther. He was appalled by the spiritual laxity and widespread abuses of ecclesiastical power he observed, sowing the seeds of his eventual break with the Church.

Lutheran Worship and Beliefs

Lutheran worship is defined as the assembly of believers where the Gospel is preached, and the Holy Sacraments are administered according to biblical teachings. The traditional liturgy closely resembles the Roman Catholic Mass and the Episcopal Church service. Initially, Lutherans retained Latin in public worship but soon transitioned to the vernacular, recognizing its value in making Scripture and liturgy accessible to all. This shift placed a stronger emphasis on preaching, which remains a central aspect of Lutheran worship today.

Lutheranism places great value on education and has, since its inception, promoted extensive Christian education programs, schools, and universities worldwide. The denomination is also deeply involved in global missions, social services, and relief efforts.

One of the hallmark doctrines of Lutheranism is the "priesthood of all believers." This teaching asserts that all Christians, regardless of gender or vocation, have the responsibility to live out and minister the teachings of Christ. The role of a pastor, derived from the Latin word for "shepherd," is not considered sacramental but is contingent upon a divine call and recognition by the congregation. Unlike Catholic clergy, Lutheran pastors may marry.

Theological Distinctions

Lutherans emphasize *sola Scriptura* ("Scripture alone"), maintaining that doctrine must be based solely on the Bible. However, they also value tradition, human reason, and the revelation of the Holy Spirit as tools for interpreting Scripture. Along with other Protestants, they uphold the doctrines of *sola gratia* ("grace alone") and *sola fide* ("faith alone"), which affirm that salvation is a free gift from God, not earned through human effort.

Luther struggled with passages like James 2:14-26, which seem to emphasize justification by works. Initially, he omitted these verses from his translation of the New Testament, leading critics to accuse him of "editing with a penknife." He later resolved the tension by interpreting the passage to mean that good works are the evidence of genuine faith rather than a means of earning salvation.

Legacy of Martin Luther

Luther's influence extended beyond theology. He challenged the seemingly unassailable power of the papacy, laying the groundwork for societal reform in Germany. His writings helped standardize the modern German language, and his emphasis on vernacular worship allowed the Gospel to reach people in their native tongues.

Salvation and the Role of Language

I believe that the Gospel should be preached in all languages, not restricted to Latin, German, or any other single tongue. Jesus came for one reason: to save humanity. Salvation encompasses all aspects of human need—physical, mental, emotional, social, and spiritual—but its core is spiritual rebirth.

God recognized that humanity could not save itself. Salvation requires a spiritual transformation, a rebirth that aligns a person's spirit with God's nature.

It is this inward renewal that enables believers to overcome the limitations of the flesh.

Conclusion

While I deeply respect the teachings of the Catholic and Lutheran traditions, I disagree with some of their doctrines. For instance, the Catholic practice of praying for the dead and belief in purgatory are not supported by my understanding of Scripture. Additionally, I question practices that seem to prioritize tradition over personal transformation and scriptural clarity.

Ultimately, faith is not about rituals or tradition alone but about a living relationship with Jesus Christ. It is through Him that we find true salvation and the strength to live according to God's will. As 2 Corinthians 5:17 reminds us:

"Therefore, if anyone is in Christ, he is a new creature; old things have passed away; behold, all things have become new."

Chapter 12

Mormonism

Faith, Revelation, and the Quest for Truth

Mormonism and Its Foundations

The Book of Mormon, according to its adherents, was written by ancient prophets under the guidance of the spirit of prophecy and revelation. These writings, inscribed on gold plates, were abridged and quoted by a prophet-historian named Mormon. After completing his work, Mormon entrusted the record to his son, Moroni, who added his own contributions before hiding the plates in the Hill Cumorah.

On September 21, 1823, Moroni, now a glorified and resurrected being, is said to have appeared to the Prophet Joseph Smith, instructing him on the record's significance and its destined translation into English. In due time, the plates were delivered to Joseph Smith, who translated them by what is described as the "gift and power of God." The resulting Book of Mormon has since been published in numerous languages and is regarded by members of the Church of Jesus Christ of Latter-day Saints (LDS Church) as an additional testament to the divinity of Jesus Christ.

Joseph Smith declared the Book of Mormon to be "the most correct of any book on earth" and the "keystone of [the LDS] religion," asserting that following its teachings would bring individuals closer to God than any other book. Beyond Smith, 11 others were chosen to bear witness to the gold plates, claiming to have seen the engravings firsthand and testifying to their authenticity.

Core Beliefs and Practices

Mormons believe their church is the true modern successor to the early church of Jesus Christ, with a mission to prepare the world for the Second Coming of Christ and the establishment of Zion. They regard the Bible as sacred but consider the Book of Mormon, the Doctrine and Covenants, and the Pearl of Great Price as equally authoritative scriptures. These additional texts include revelations given to Joseph Smith and writings attributed to Abraham and Moses.

Central tenets of Mormonism include continuous revelation from God, faith in Jesus Christ, repentance, baptism by immersion for the remission of sins, and the laying on of hands for the gift of the Holy Ghost. Mormons also practice a form of communion with bread and water, reflecting their emphasis on simplicity and accessibility in worship.

The LDS Church places great importance on health, education, and self-reliance. Members are encouraged to abstain from alcohol, tobacco, coffee, and tea, and recreation is considered an essential part of life. The church operates a robust welfare program and discourages reliance on public aid, instead promoting tithing as a means of supporting the community.

Historical Context

Founded by Joseph Smith in 1830, the LDS Church quickly grew in numbers, attracting both followers and controversy. Smith claimed that at the age of 14, he began receiving visions, including a visit from God the Father and Jesus Christ. In 1827, he announced the discovery of golden plates inscribed with hieroglyphics, which he translated with divine assistance to produce the Book of Mormon.

The church's early history was marked by migration and persecution. Members moved westward to Utah in search of religious freedom, enduring significant hardships in the process. Despite their efforts to isolate themselves and achieve economic self-sufficiency, the Mormons faced challenges from external influences and internal reforms, including the eventual abandonment of plural marriage.

Conclusion

While the LDS Church emphasizes faith, community, and moral values, critics—including myself—have raised concerns about its exclusivity and truth claims. The assertion that the Mormon Church possesses "more truth" than other faiths and its use of fear-based tactics to maintain membership have led some to view it as a controlling institution.

I personally believe in a God of unconditional love, whose presence permeates the universe. Great spiritual teachers, including Jesus, Buddha, and Mohammed, have provided valuable guidance on how to reconnect with the divine and fulfill our highest potential. However, I do not subscribe to the idea that any one religion, including Mormonism, holds a monopoly on truth or access to God.

Religion should inspire individuals to grow spiritually and morally, without coercion or exclusivity. True faith is not about fear or control but about love, understanding, and the freedom to seek one's own connection with the divine.

Chapter 13

The Puritans

Pioneers of Faith, Reform, and Society

The Puritans: Reformers of Faith and Society

O riginally, Puritans were those who sought to "purify" the Church of England of practices and beliefs not explicitly based on the Bible. Emerging during the Reformation, Puritanism initially aimed to reform doctrine and ritual but evolved into a political and social movement that shaped the history of England and New England.

Puritans belonged to the Calvinist reform movement and rejected elements of the Church of England's practices, which they viewed as rooted in Catholic tradition. They opposed practices such as making the sign of the cross, kneeling during Holy Communion, clergy vestments, and ornate church decorations.

Original Sin and Salvation by Grace

The Puritans embraced Calvinistic doctrines, including the belief in original sin—the inherited guilt from Adam's fall in Eden. They also emphasized salvation by grace alone, rejecting the idea that good works or sacraments could redeem humanity. This theology stressed God's sovereignty and the inability of humans to save themselves.

Moral Conduct and Piety

Puritanism demanded strict personal morality and piety in daily life. They condemned forms of entertainment such as dancing, theater, and gambling, viewing worldly pleasures as distractions from godliness. Instead, virtues like self-reliance, frugality, and hard work were upheld as marks of a faithful life.

Church Government and Division

Initially, most Puritans sought to reform the Church of England's doctrine and ritual without separating from it. However, disagreements over governance and theology led to divisions:

1. **Presbyterianism**: Advocated for governance by elected elders rather than bishops.

2. **Congregationalism**: Favored self-governing congregations independent of higher church authorities.

3. **Separatists**: The most radical faction, advocating full separation from the Church of England.

By the end of the 16th century, these divisions deepened as Puritans faced increasing persecution under the Stuart monarchy.

Persecution and Migration: Persecution in England

Under the Stuarts, beginning in 1603, Puritans faced harassment. Persecution intensified after William Laud became the head of the Church of England in 1633, leading many Puritans to flee to Holland and later to the New World.

Migration to New England

Puritan settlement in New England began with the Pilgrims, Separatists who founded Plymouth Colony in 1620. The majority of Puritans, however, established the Massachusetts Bay Colony a few years later. These settlers were primarily Congregationalists who sought to build churches free from Anglican control.

In New England, the Puritans envisioned a "city on a hill," a godly community where all aspects of life aligned with biblical principles. Their society regulated everything from trade practices to personal behavior, aiming to create a unified, morally upright community.

Factors Supporting Puritan Society

1. Religious Vision: Inspired by biblical prophecies and shaped by persecution, Puritans sought to honor God in every aspect of life.

2. Demographic Composition: Unlike other colonies populated by young men seeking fortune, Puritan migration typically consisted of stable family units with relatively educated parents.

3. Massachusetts Charter: Negotiated by John Winthrop in 1629, this charter allowed the colony an unprecedented degree of autonomy from England, fostering the Puritan vision of a communal utopia.

Challenges and Decline

Over time, however, the Puritan dream of a unified godly community began to wane:

- Generational Divide: Younger generations, lacking the formative experiences of persecution in England, were less focused on religious ideals.

- Economic Focus: Increasing attention to trade and private wealth diluted the community's spiritual priorities.

- Religious Tolerance: The 1662 Half-Way Covenant attempted to address divisions by allowing partial church membership, but it highlighted growing fractures. By 1691, Massachusetts' new royal charter reduced Puritan authority and increased religious tolerance.

By 1700, New England retained its distinct Puritan character but could no longer replicate the fervent religious zeal of its first settlers.

Puritan Views on Church and State

The Puritans' understanding of the relationship between church and state contrasts sharply with modern American principles. While the U.S. government is prohibited from promoting any particular faith, the Puritans believed church and government should work together to promote holiness and ensure both material and spiritual success.

This integration of church and state aimed to create a society that honored God in all aspects of life. However, the strict moral and religious demands of Puritan leaders, coupled with their intolerance of dissent, contributed to their eventual decline in influence.

Legacy and Misunderstanding

The Puritans are often misunderstood, in part due to their reputation for intolerance and legalism. While they were human and prone to the same weaknesses as all people, their dedication to serving God wholeheartedly cannot be overlooked.

Modern secular perspectives often dismiss the Puritans, failing to grasp the joy and satisfaction they found in their faith. As a result, their contributions to American culture—emphasizing hard work, education, and moral responsibility—are sometimes overshadowed by criticism of their rigidity.

Conclusion

The Puritans' vision of a godly society, their emphasis on faith and morality, and their unique approach to governance left a lasting imprint on both England and America. Though their dream of a unified community ultimately proved unsustainable, their dedication to living according to biblical principles continues to inspire and challenge modern understandings of faith and society.

Chapter 14

Understanding Roman Catholicism

The Universal Church

The Largest Christian Denomination

R oman Catholicism is the largest of Christianity's three major branches, the others being the Eastern Orthodox Church and Protestantism. The schism between the Catholic and Orthodox Churches began in the fourth century, when the Roman Empire divided, and became final in 1054. For centuries, the Roman Catholic Church was the dominant force in Western Europe, serving as a unifying institution during tumultuous periods. At times, the pope wielded significant authority, even disciplining civil rulers. Protestantism later emerged in the 16th century during the Reformation, challenging the Catholic Church's dominance.

Today, over one billion Christians identify as Catholic, making up more than half of the global Christian population. In the United States alone, Roman Catholics number approximately 49 million, out of a total Christian population of 128 million.

Core Beliefs and Doctrines

Catholics believe that the principal truths of their faith were revealed by God and have been passed down unchanged through the church established by Christ. These truths are derived from two main sources: the Bible and Sacred Tradition—the oral teachings of the apostles and their successors. While the Pope, as the church's supreme leader, may clarify doctrines, he cannot add to or subtract from the core articles of faith.

The central tenets of Catholicism are summarized in four creeds, the most well-known being the Apostles' Creed and the Nicene Creed. The Apostles' Creed, rooted in the teachings of the apostles, dates back to the second century.

Authority of the Church

Catholics hold that their church is of divine origin, established by Jesus Christ when he declared to Saint Peter, "Thou art Peter, and upon this rock I will build my church" (Matthew 16:18). They view Peter as the foundation of the church and the first pope. His authority, granted by Christ, is believed to have been passed down to his successors. The Pope, as Peter's successor, is the visible head of the church on Earth, sharing governance with the bishops, who are seen as the successors to the apostles.

The doctrine of papal infallibility holds that the Pope cannot err when officially defining doctrines of faith and morals. However, this infallibility is limited to spiritual matters and does not extend to his personal opinions or actions.

The Seven Sacraments

The religious life of Catholics centers on seven sacraments, which they believe were instituted by Jesus Christ and serve as conduits of divine grace:

1. **Baptism**: Cleanses the soul of sin and initiates the individual into the church.

2. **Confirmation**: Strengthens the baptized person through the anointing of the Holy Spirit.

3. **Eucharist (Holy Communion)**: Bread and wine are transformed into the body and blood of Christ, nourishing the soul.

4. **Penance**: Offers forgiveness for sins through confession and absolution.

5. **Anointing of the Sick**: Provides healing and comfort for the seriously ill or dying.

6. **Holy Orders**: Ordains individuals to serve as deacons, priests, or bishops.

7. **Matrimony**: Sanctifies the union of a man and woman in marriage.

Devotion to Saints and Mary

Catholics venerate saints as models of virtuous living and often seek their intercession in prayer. The Blessed Virgin Mary holds a special place in Catholic devotion. Catholics honor her as the Mother of God and believe she intercedes on their behalf with her Son, Jesus Christ. Images and statues of Mary and the saints are revered, not as objects of worship but as reminders of their exemplary lives.

Controversial Beliefs and Practices

Some Catholic practices, such as praying for the dead and the doctrine of purgatory, have been sources of theological debate. Purgatory is believed to be a temporary state where souls are purified before entering heaven. Catholics also uphold clerical celibacy as a discipline for priests, believing it allows them to fully dedicate their lives to God.

While the church's sacraments and sacramentals—holy water, crucifixes, rosaries, and other blessed items—are meant to inspire devotion, they have at times been misunderstood as superstitious objects. The church emphasizes that these items are spiritual aids, not magical talismans.

The Reformation and Modern Challenges

The Protestant Reformation of the 16th century, led by figures like Martin Luther, arose partly in response to perceived corruption and worldliness within the Catholic Church. The Council of Trent (1545–1563) marked the Catholic Counter-Reformation, reaffirming Catholic doctrines and addressing abuses. While the Reformation led to significant changes in Christendom, the Catholic Church remains steadfast in its traditions and teachings.

Reflections and Personal Perspectives

As an observer, I recognize the deep history and widespread influence of the Catholic Church. However, I also hold differing views on some of its doctrines and practices. For instance, I do not align with the concept of purgatory or the veneration of saints and Mary as intermediaries between believers and God. Additionally, I question cultural practices such as indulgent celebrations that may conflict with biblical teachings on living a godly life.

Galatians 5:13 reminds us, *"Brethren, ye have been called unto liberty; only use not liberty for an occasion to the flesh, but by love serve one another."* This verse underscores the importance of living in alignment with spiritual values rather than worldly indulgences.

Conclusion

The Roman Catholic Church has undeniably shaped the spiritual, cultural, and historical landscape of the world. While it remains a source of profound faith and devotion for millions, its traditions and doctrines continue to inspire dialogue and reflection among believers and non-believers alike. By exploring its teachings and practices, we gain a deeper understanding of the enduring role of faith in human history and the complexities of religious belief in the modern world.

Chapter 15

Unitarianism

Faith Without Boundaries

Unitarianism: A Distinctive Perspective on Christianity

Historically, Unitarians differ from mainstream Christianity most notably in their rejection of the doctrine of the Trinity and their denial that Jesus is God. Like many Christian offshoots, Unitarians claim to adhere more closely to the original truths of Christianity, which they believe were lost in the early Church councils. In theological terms, Unitarianism aligns most closely with Arianism, which posited that the Son is subordinate to the Father, though Unitarians generally go further in denying the deity of Christ.

Unitarianism shares common ground with various intellectual and religious movements, including the Deists and Freethinkers of the 18th century, Universalists of the same era, the secular Utilitarianism of the 19th century, and the Modernists who embraced biblical criticism. This free-thinking tradition has often drawn condemnation from more orthodox Christian groups, particularly Evangelicals, who view Unitarianism as a heretical movement.

A "Thinking Person's Religion"

In America, Unitarianism has historically been regarded as intellectually and socially progressive, often referred to as "the thinking man's religion." Critics have described it as humanism with a spiritual foundation or a religion for the religious skeptic. This intellectual openness was further bolstered in 1961 when the Universalist Church of America merged with the American Unitarian Association, forming the Unitarian Universalist Association (UUA). Today, the UUA has approximately 200,000 members in the United States.

Beliefs and Practices

One of the most distinctive aspects of Unitarianism is its rejection of creeds. While many Unitarians share similar beliefs, they emphasize freedom of thought and worship, resisting any attempt to impose a uniform doctrine. This commitment to pluralism is central to their identity, as reflected in their acceptance of diverse perspectives, from liberal Christianity to religious humanism.

As one Unitarian put it:

"The main point of division between Unitarians and mainstream Christianity is our welcome acceptance of religious pluralism, encompassing a broad spectrum of views, such that some members think of themselves more as religious humanists rather than Christians." (Barrett, 1996, p. 54)

Despite this diversity, there is general agreement on certain core beliefs:

- **God as One:** Unitarians affirm the oneness of God and reject the Trinitarian concept of God as Father, Son, and Holy Spirit.

- **Jesus as Human:** They believe Jesus was a man—a holy and exemplary one—but not divine. The Church Fathers, in their view, transformed the historical Jesus into the God-man of Trinitarian theology.

- **No Atonement Doctrine:** Jesus' death on the cross is seen as an act of love and sacrifice, not as atonement for humanity's sins.

Unitarians value insights from other world religions, science, and reason, making their faith an ever-evolving blend of Jewish and Christian roots with a global perspective.

Social Activism and Inclusivity

Unitarians have long been pioneers in social reform. They were the first denomination in Britain to appoint professional women ministers in 1904, and they actively fight against discrimination based on race, gender, or sexual orientation. Their churches openly welcome LGBTQ+ individuals and advocate for their legal and social rights.

Congregational governance is a hallmark of Unitarianism. Each congregation is independent and self-governing, with no centralized authority dictating doctrine or practice. This decentralized structure reflects their commitment to individual freedom and collective responsibility.

Historical Challenges

Unitarianism has faced significant challenges throughout its history. In England, the Act of Uniformity of 1662 imposed strict regulations on who could preach and what could be preached, effectively excluding Unitarians. While the Act of Toleration in 1689 granted some freedoms to other Nonconformist groups, Unitarians remained marginalized. Nevertheless, their teachings continued to influence congregations and individuals, particularly as they sought to reconcile biblical faith with emerging scientific discoveries.

In the United States, Unitarianism played a central role in intellectual and social life. Harvard College became a hub for Unitarian thought, and prominent figures like Thomas Jefferson and John Quincy Adams embraced Unitarian beliefs.

Contemporary Challenges

Despite its rich history and progressive values, Unitarianism faces challenges in the modern era. With its emphasis on individualism and pluralism, the movement struggles to maintain a cohesive identity. Membership numbers are relatively small, and critics argue that the lack of a unified creed makes it difficult for the movement to grow and sustain itself.

As one critic notes, "The Unitarian religion is disappearing little by little because they lack a strong foundation in their beliefs." While this perspective may not fully account for the adaptability and resilience of Unitarianism, it underscores the challenges of sustaining a faith tradition rooted in individual freedom and diverse interpretations.

Conclusion

Unitarianism represents a unique approach to faith, blending intellectual rigor, social activism, and religious pluralism. Its rejection of dogma and embrace of diversity offer a refreshing alternative to more rigid traditions, but these same qualities present challenges for long-term growth and cohesion.

As a liberal religious movement, Unitarianism continues to advocate for inclusivity, equality, and dialogue, striving to remain relevant in an ever-changing world. Whether it thrives or diminishes, its legacy as a pioneer of free thought and progressive values remains a significant contribution to religious history.

Chapter 16

Sikh

The Journey to Spiritual Liberation

Curiosity and the Study of Religion: The Sikh Perspective

Curiosity often drives the study of different cultures and religions, as people seek to understand practices that intrigue the imagination or dominate media headlines. Religions that have recently gained attention in the West are particularly concerned with how they are portrayed. For Sikhs, this concern arises from being unfairly branded as militant or extremist—a stereotype that obscures the essence of their deeply spiritual and philosophical traditions.

At its core, Sikhism teaches that the universe is God's creation, operating in perfect obedience to divine will. For Sikhs, there is no question about whether this is the best possible world—it unequivocally is, as it reflects the will of a perfect Creator.

Human Distinctiveness and Potential

The Sikh Gurus emphasized human distinctiveness and the immense potential granted to humankind, setting it apart from the rest of creation:

1. **Discrimination and Choice:** Humans have the unique ability to discern between good and bad and to make meaningful choices.

2. **Moral Agency:** Earnings and resources can be directed toward selfish ends, personal improvement, or altruistic purposes.

3. **Union with God:** Humans have the extraordinary potential to consciously unite with God, a privilege granted through divine grace.

However, this potential is often unrealized because many people are unaware of God's presence in their lives or outright deny His existence.

The Struggle with Haumai and Maya

Sikhism identifies the root of human struggles as **haumai**, or self-reliance. This "I-am-ness" blinds people to their dependence on God and reduces their spiritual understanding. Guru Nanak taught that haumai leads to attachment to worldly values and behaviors that alienate individuals from their divine nature.

The Concept of Maya

In Sikh philosophy, **maya** represents worldly attachment rather than illusion. It encompasses both acceptable and destructive attachments, such as devotion to family, patriotism, or material wealth, which can divert attention from God. The five evils—lust (kam), greed (lobh), attachment (moh), anger (krodh), and pride (ahankar)—are manifestations of haumai that distort human relationships and priorities.

As Guru Nanak explained:

"The love of worldly values stretches over the whole world. Seeing a beautiful woman, a man covets her. With his sons and gold, man increases his love. He considers everything to be his own. He does not heed God."

Maya, therefore, becomes a test of human discrimination and choice, presenting opportunities for attachment to worldly distractions or devotion to God.

Liberation through Grace and Effort

The Sikh path to liberation involves shifting from self-centeredness to God-centeredness. This transformation requires human effort, divine grace, and active engagement with spiritual teachings.

Stories of Transformation

The Sikh tradition is rich with stories illustrating the power of spiritual awakening. One such story is that of **Sajjan**, a deceitful man who lured travelers to his inn, only to rob and kill them. When Guru Nanak and his companion Mardana visited Sajjan, they sang hymns throughout the night. These hymns stirred Sajjan's conscience, leading him to repent and seek Guru Nanak's guidance. Sajjan not only reformed his life but also paid restitution to his victims' families, built a dharamsala (an early form of gurdwara), and gave his wealth to the poor.

This story highlights key Sikh principles:

1. **The Transformative Power of Bani:** Listening to sacred hymns can inspire profound change.

2. **Divine Grace and Human Effort:** While Sajjan needed divine grace for enlightenment, his sincere desire to change and take responsibility for his actions was essential.

3. **A Transformed Life:** True spiritual enlightenment manifests in actions that reflect compassion, humility, and service to others.

The Role of Grace

Guru Nanak emphasized that while good actions may lead to a human form, liberation is a gift of divine grace:

"Good actions may result in a human form, but liberation comes only from God's grace. God cannot be won through rites or deeds. Learning cannot help in comprehending God. That comes only from the True God."

Conclusion

Sikh teachings offer practical guidance for achieving spiritual liberation:

1. **Naam Simran (Meditation on God's Name):** Constant remembrance of God fosters a God-centered life.

2. **Seva (Selfless Service):** Serving others without expectation cultivates humility and detachment from haumai.

3. **Sangat (Community):** Participation in the holy congregation reinforces shared values and mutual support.

4. **Kirtan (Singing Hymns):** Devotional music connects individuals with divine grace.

By reorienting life toward God, individuals can overcome the illusions of maya and haumai, achieving a state of spiritual liberation while still engaged in the world.

Chapter 17

Sufism

Exploring the Heart of Devine Unity

Initial Thoughts

C uriosity often drives the study of culture and religion. For many, religions attract attention due to their distinct practices, captivating headlines, or portrayal in the media. This exposure often shapes perceptions, particularly when misunderstandings arise. For Sikhs, media coverage has sometimes branded them as militant fanatics, overshadowing the essence of their spiritual teachings.

At the core of Sikh belief is the conviction that the universe is God's creation, operating in perfect accordance with divine will. For Sikhs, there is no question about whether this is the best possible world—God, as the perfect Creator, has ensured that it is.

Human Potential in Sikh Teachings

The Sikh Gurus focused on humanity's potential and destiny, steering away from metaphysical distractions to address practical spiritual concerns. They taught that humans are distinct within creation due to certain unique traits:

1. **Moral Discrimination**: Humans possess the ability to discern between good and bad, making choices that reflect their values.

2. **Intentional Action**: Resources and actions can be directed toward selfishness, personal improvement, or altruistic causes.

3. **Union with God**: Unlike other creatures, humans have the opportunity to consciously unite with God through their choices.

Yet, despite these capabilities, many fail to recognize God's presence in their lives. The Gurus reminded their followers:

"You are blessed by being born human; it is an opportunity to meet your God."

Human ignorance, they emphasized, stems from materialist views of the universe and a self-centered approach to life, which Guru Nanak termed *haumai* (self-reliance or "I-am-ness"). This condition blinds individuals to their dependence on God and reduces them to the level of animals driven by instinct.

The Challenge of *Haumai*

Haumai distorts human priorities, leading to attachment to worldly values (*maya*). While the created world is not an illusion, as some Hindu philosophies propose, *maya* refers to an unhealthy attachment to the temporal world. Even socially acceptable attachments—such as love for family or patriotism—can become distractions from the ultimate devotion to God.

The Sikh Gurus identified five evils rooted in *haumai*: lust (*kam*), covetousness (*lobh*), attachment (*moh*), wrath (*krodh*), and pride (*ahankar*). Each represents a quality that, when unchecked, leads to spiritual degradation. Guru Nanak described this distortion:

"The love of worldly values stretches over the whole world. Seeing a beautiful woman, a man covets her. With his sons and gold, man increases his love. He considers everything to be his own. He does not heed God."

Despite these pitfalls, Sikhism teaches that liberation is attainable. By overcoming *haumai* and reorienting oneself toward God, individuals can experience spiritual freedom even within the constraints of *maya*.

The Role of Grace and Effort

Sikh teachings emphasize that liberation ultimately depends on God's grace, though human effort plays a significant role. The story of Sajjan, a wealthy but corrupt innkeeper, exemplifies this interplay. Sajjan lured travelers to his inn, offering shelter and places of worship, only to rob and kill them. However, when Guru Nanak and his companion Mardana visited, their hymns pierced Sajjan's heart. Struck by their message, Sajjan repented, gave away his wealth to the poor, and built the first *gurdwara* (then called a *dharamsala*).

This story highlights key Sikh principles:

- **The Transformative Power of *Bani***: Sacred hymns have the capacity to awaken and transform.

- **Divine Grace**: Enlightenment is made possible through God's intervention.

- **Human Effort**: Sincere desire and action are necessary for lasting change.

- **Spiritual Transformation**: True liberation manifests in ethical, compassionate living.

Guru Nanak taught:

"Good actions may result in a human form, but liberation comes only from God's grace. God cannot be won through rites or deeds. Learning cannot help in comprehending God. That comes only from the True God."

Maya and Liberation

The Sikh understanding of *maya* goes beyond material wealth to encompass any attachment that diverts attention from God. The path to liberation involves reversing this attachment and becoming God-centered. While human effort initiates this journey, divine grace completes it.

Even in the midst of *maya*, individuals can experience divine presence. Guru Nanak proclaimed:

"Those who enshrine love for God in their hearts, through the Guru's grace, obtain God even in the midst of maya."

Conclusion

Sikhism provides a clear and practical path to spiritual liberation. By moving away from *haumai* and aligning oneself with divine will, humans can fulfill their unique potential and achieve unity with God. The teachings of the Sikh Gurus challenge individuals to recognize the transient nature of worldly attachments and embrace a life of devotion, service, and humility. In doing so, they find liberation not only in the hereafter but also within the complexities of earthly existence.

Chapter 18

Faith, Secularism, and the Quest for Security

Navigating Belief in Modern Times

Faith, Secularism, and the Search for Security

In recent times, assumptions about faith and religion have come under scrutiny. It was once widely presumed that those who abandoned Christianity would naturally align themselves with another recognized religion, such as Hinduism or Islam, or at least adopt some form of belief system akin to faith. However, the contemporary world has seen a growing number of individuals living comfortably without any semblance of faith, religious or otherwise.

This raises critical questions: Is faith still a universal human need? Or has it become an obsolete concept in the face of secularism, materialism, and modernity?

Defining Faith

Our understanding of this issue hinges on how we define "faith." The Apostle Paul contrasts "walking by faith" with "walking by sight" (*2 Corinthians 5:7*). Faith pertains to the unseen but is no less real for being intangible. Sight, in this context, refers to observable phenomena, things that can be measured, tested, and intellectually grasped.

Modern secularists often equate faith with blind acceptance—belief in something unsupported by evidence or reason. This misunderstanding positions faith as an irrational leap, detached from reality. Consequently, many associate faith with outdated traditions or mere fantasies. Christians themselves have sometimes contributed to this misconception by failing to articulate what faith truly entails.

Faith, properly understood, is not antithetical to reason. It is a trust in the unseen truths of God's promises, supported by historical witness, spiritual experience, and the inner testimony of the Holy Spirit.

Secularism and the Challenge to Faith

The rise of secularism represents a significant challenge to faith. Modern secularism often prides itself on being "scientific," grounded in empirical evidence and rational inquiry. This worldview dismisses faith as antiquated, associating it with superstition or oppressive traditions.

Marxism and Religion

Marxism, another challenge to faith, views religion as a vestige of the capitalist past. Karl Marx, though a baptized Jew well-acquainted with Christianity, regarded religion as a tool of oppression. He predicted that the advancement of science and the proletarian revolution would lead to religion's eventual demise.

In Marxist doctrine, all religions—including Christianity, Judaism, and Islam—are seen as impediments to social and economic progress. Religion is tolerated only if confined strictly to private worship and removed entirely from social, political, or economic matters.

Marxism's Paradoxical Connection to Christianity

Despite its hostility toward religion, Marxism echoes certain Christian values and teachings. Marx emphasized the importance of addressing material realities, such as poverty and inequality—concerns central to Jesus' ministry. While Christ taught that "man shall not live by bread alone," he never discounted the necessity of bread (*Matthew 4:4*). His command, "Give ye them to eat" (*Luke 9:13*), underscores the Church's responsibility to care for both the physical and spiritual needs of humanity.

Marxist ideals, such as the pursuit of human dignity and the restoration of a just society, resonate with Christian teachings. However, Marx's vision diverged significantly in its methods and ultimate goals. His revolutionary approach often dismissed compassion and individual dignity, focusing instead on the inevitable triumph of proletarian forces.

Marx himself was a contentious figure—angry, authoritarian, and often at odds with his associates. His interest in social conditions, by his own admission, was driven more by scientific analysis than by compassion. Nevertheless, Christians can agree with his critique of societal injustices and his insistence on the need for systemic change, even if they reject his means and materialist worldview.

The Christian Response to Marxism

Christianity provides a broader and more hopeful vision than Marxism. Where Marxism offers a utopian vision of a human-engineered future, Christianity points to the Kingdom of God—a realm of justice, peace, and reconciliation achieved not by human effort alone but through divine grace.

The Christian message emphasizes the inherent dignity of every individual, created in the image of God. It calls for action to address social and economic inequalities, guided by love and compassion rather than ideological dogma.

The Universal Search for Security

In today's world, the search for security is universal. People seek it in various forms:

- **Women** look to husbands as providers.

- **Men** seek stability in their careers.

- **The elderly** yearn for secure homes and companionship.

- **Children** find security in family and parental love.

- **Businesspeople** trust in financial investments.

While these forms of security are important, they are ultimately transient. True security comes from a relationship with God. Psalm 91 declares:

"I will say of the Lord, He is my refuge and my fortress: my God; in him will I trust." (Psalm 91:2)

God's promises of protection and provision offer a foundation that transcends the uncertainties of life. In Him, we find a refuge that withstands the storms of a changing world.

Conclusion

In a world increasingly defined by secularism and skepticism, faith remains a vital and transformative force. It provides meaning and purpose beyond material realities, anchoring individuals in the eternal truths of God's love and grace.

Faith challenges the assumption that humanity can find fulfillment in material progress alone. It calls us to recognize our dependence on God and to live lives marked by love, service, and hope.

As the Apostle Paul reminds us:

"If God be for us, who can be against us?" (Romans 8:31)

In this truth lies the ultimate security—not in fleeting human constructs, but in the eternal promises of God.

Chapter 19

Threads of the Divine

Exploring Uniqueness and Unity in World
Religions

Initial Thoughts

I t is often stated that each religion is unique. For instance, Christians emphasize the uniqueness of Christ. While it is essential to acknowledge such
claims, it is equally important not to overstate them. As unique individuals,
we still share similarities that allow for meaningful comparisons—whether it be
between physical traits like noses or universal experiences like heartbeats. Similarly, religions, despite their differences, exhibit overlapping features that can aid
us in understanding and appreciating diverse faiths. For example, recognizing
similarities between Mahayana meditation and Christian contemplation can
foster a more positive and open attitude between adherents of these traditions.

Mysticism and Contemplation Across Religions

Mysticism, or contemplation, offers one of the most intriguing points of com-
parison among religions. Some scholars argue that mystical experiences across
traditions share a common core (e.g., Evelyn Underhill and Friedrich von
Hügel). Others contend that contextual differences result in fundamentally
different experiences. However, this debate may overlook the fact that universal

human experiences, like love or fear, can vary culturally without losing their core essence.

For instance, the contemplative experiences of a Chinese Buddhist and a Muslim Sufi may differ in cultural framing, but their inner transformation and sense of transcendence may share striking similarities. Furthermore, theistic mysticism—seen in Christian, Sufi, Jewish Kabbalistic, and Hindu Yogic traditions—often centers on a personal relationship with the Divine, while non-theistic mysticism, such as Theravada Buddhist meditation, emphasizes the dissolution of the self. Even within theistic mysticism, an impersonal aspect often arises, as traditions grapple with the ineffable nature of God.

The Ineffable and the Shared Mystical Core

The unutterable nature of mystical experiences is a recurring theme in many traditions. Christianity, for instance, draws on Neo-Platonist motifs to describe God as indescribable and beyond human comprehension. Similar ideas appear in Sufi, Hindu, and Jewish mysticism, suggesting a shared acknowledgment of divine ineffability.

Some scholars argue that this ineffability bridges theistic and non-theistic mysticism, as both grapple with realities beyond language. However, the paths leading to such experiences—the "tunnels" through which individuals approach the "light"—may color the perception of the destination. For theistic contemplatives, the journey often involves devotion and prophecy, while non-theistic contemplatives pursue purity and detachment. Despite these differences, the light itself may be fundamentally the same.

The Numinous and Mystical Experiences

Religious experience is not limited to contemplation. The numinous, as described by Rudolf Otto, is another key dimension, marked by a sense of the "wholly Other" that inspires both awe and fascination. Otto's examples—Arjuna's vision in the *Bhagavad Gita*, Job's encounter with God in the whirlwind, and Paul's conversion on the Damascus road—illustrate the numinous across traditions.

While mystical and numinous experiences overlap, they differ in focus. The numinous emphasizes God's otherness, while mysticism seeks union with the Divine. This distinction underscores the diversity within religious experiences, even as commonalities emerge.

Ethical Convergences and Divergences

Despite theological and ritual differences, major religions often converge on ethical principles. The Golden Rule, ideas of compassion, brotherhood, and love, and prohibitions against harm and deceit are widely shared. Yet differences persist: for example, views on reincarnation, dietary laws, and moral issues like homosexuality and abortion vary across traditions.

Rebirth or reincarnation, central to Hinduism and Buddhism, contrasts sharply with the eschatological focus of Abrahamic religions. Similarly, interpretations of moral principles—such as adultery or truth-telling—can differ even within a single tradition.

Toward a Global Ethos

Religions often diverge on questions of revelation, ritual, and doctrine, yet their shared ethical values suggest a foundation for mutual understanding. Recognizing these overlaps can help bridge divides and encourage the development of a global ethos. Such reflection is essential as we navigate the pluralism of our world and seek frameworks for coexistence.

Conclusion

In exploring the overlaps and differences among religions, it becomes clear that while traditions retain their unique characteristics, they also share profound commonalities. These resemblances—whether in contemplative practices, ethical principles, or the sense of the Divine—invite us to engage with diverse faiths thoughtfully. By focusing on these shared elements, we can foster greater interfaith understanding and perhaps even work toward a universal ethic. Moving forward, the challenge lies in discerning how to judge the teachings and practices of various traditions as we seek wisdom in a diverse spiritual landscape.

Chapter 20

The Evolution of Religious Choice and Its Role in Modern Society

In Conclusion

In the past, religion was often an unchosen inheritance, determined by geography, culture, and state power. Societal cohesion frequently depended on religious unity, with governments using religion as a tool to legitimize authority and maintain order. In such a framework, individual choice played a negligible role; adherence to a faith was more a matter of practicality and tradition than personal conviction.

However, the modern world presents a vastly different landscape. In the Protestant West and increasingly across the globe, religion has shifted from a communal, state-supported institution to a personal, private matter. Today, individuals are free to choose—or reject—religion, and many do so. Secularism, with its focus on the here and now rather than the hereafter, has become the prevailing orthodoxy of governance, influencing societal norms and values.

Religious institutions now operate in a marketplace of ideas where belief systems must resonate with personal experiences, provide meaningful answers, and demonstrate a God or spiritual force with the power to act. For many, the concept of a deity has been rendered inert—either unreal or incapable of influencing a world perceived as dominated by secular forces. This has led to a decline in traditional religious authority and the rise of agnosticism, atheism, and vague spiritualities that require little to no commitment.

Modern secular governance has stripped religion of its political authority, embracing pluralism and condemning discrimination based on faith. This has brought many benefits, such as the disappearance of religious tests for public office, the decline of censorship, and a more inclusive approach to societal organization. Yet, it has also left governments grappling with responsibilities previously attributed to divine will—planning for societal well-being and bearing the brunt of blame when things go awry.

While these changes are welcomed by many, they also present challenges for religious institutions. In a world where belief is no longer inherited but chosen, religions must adapt to meet the spiritual and existential needs of modern individuals. This demands a reimagining of faith that transcends dogma, engages with contemporary issues, and reaffirms its relevance in a rapidly changing world.

Ultimately, the shift toward personal religious choice reflects broader societal transformations: the rise of individualism, the decentralization of authority, and the quest for meaning in a secular age. This evolution is not merely a loss for traditional religion but an opportunity to redefine its role in fostering personal and collective well-being in a pluralistic world.

Bibliography

Armstrong Karen: Islam (The Prophet, p.45)

International and Pan-American, Published in the United States by Random House, Inc,

New York, and simultaneously in Canada; printed in the United States of America, 2000

Barrett David V.: Sect,' Cults' & Alternative Religion; (Unitarians, p.54)

Published in the UK, 1996 by Bland ford A Chassell Imprint CASSL PLC Wellington House 125 Strand London WC2R 0BB

Bonwick James: Irish Oruios Ano Olo Irish Religions. (Early Religion of the Irish, p.76) Published by Dorset Press 1986; Dorset Press, Printed in the United States of America

Bushman Lauper Claudia and Bushman Lyman Richard: Building the Kingdom, (The Church since 1823, p.88) Published by Oxford University Press, Inc

198 Madison Avenue, New York, New York 10016 printed, 1999

Cavolina Frances Jane Mary, Stone Joseph Allen Jeffrey, and Kelly Teresa Anne Maureen Davis Michael Glenn Richard: Growing up Catholic (The Sacramental, p.108) First Broadway Books trade paperback edition published, 2000. Printed in the United States of America

Cavendish Richard: The Great Religions, (Judaism, p.133) Published by Arco Publishing, Inc; 219 Park Avenue South, New York, N.Y. 10003 Printed in Italy, 1980

Cole Owen W: Sikhism, world faiths (Human Nature and Spiritual Liberation p.126) Published in 1994 NTC Publishing Group, 4255 West Touhy Avenue, Lincolnwood (Chicago), Illinois. Printed and bound in Great Britain by Cox & Wyman Ltd.

Coleman William James: The New Buddhism, (Practice and Belief, p.91) Published by Oxford University Press Inc, 198 Madison Avenue New York 10016 2001

Dudley, William and Teresa O'Neill: Puritanism (Creating a Godly Community, p.120), 1994 by Greenhaven Press, Inc., PO Box 289009, San Diego, CA 92198-9009 printed in the U.S.A.

Elide Mircea & Couliane Ioan P.: World Religions, (Egyptian Religion, p.1 02) Printed in United States of America; Harper Collins Publishers, 10East 53rd Street New York, NY10022, 1989

Holden Andrew: Jehovah's Witnesses; (Honor they father and they mother, p. 125). Simultaneously published in the USA and Canada by Rutledge; 29Weest 35th Street New York, NY 10001 printed, 2002

Knight, Sirona: Citric Traditions (Celtic Gods and Goddesses, p.37) Kensington Published by 850 Third Avenue New York NY 10022 Printing in the United States of America, 2000

Klostermaier klaus K.: Hinduism (the modern Hinduism, p.231) Oneworld Publications (US Marketing Office) 160 N. Washington St. 4th Floor, Boston MA 02114 USA Printed and bound in England by Clays Ltd, St Ives ;plc, 2000

Losch, Richard R.: The Many Faces of Faith; (The Lutherans, p.93) Wm. B. Eerdmans Publishing Co. 255 Jefferson S.E. Grand Rapids Michigan; Printed in the United States of America, 2001

Neill, Stephen Charles, Christian Faith and other Faith, New York Oxford University press 1970, printed in Great Britain

Saunders George R. Culture and Christianity: (the Origins of Revival, a Creole

Religion in Jamaica, p. 91) published in 1988, Greenwood Press, Inc. 88 Post Road West Westport printed in the United States of America

Shea David and Troyer Anthony: The Religion of the Sufis

Published for the Sufis Trust by The Octagon Press, Printed and Bound in Great Britain by Tonbridge Printers Ltd., Tonbridge, Kent (1979, P.27)

Smart Ninian: Choosing A Faith, (How Religions May Agree p.42)

Published in 1995 by Bowerdean Publishing Co, Ltd., 8 Abbotstone Rd, London SW15 1QR AND Marion Boyars Publishers, 24 Lacy Rd., London SW15 1NL and 237 East 39th St., New York, NY 10016

Smylie James H.: A brief history of the Presbyterians (The birth of the reformed tradition in Europe, p.15) Published by Geneva Press Louisville, Kentucky; Printed in the United States of America, 199

Torode Sam and Bethany: (who is a Christian) website

Christianity today magazine print in the USA 11/12/ 2001

www.ingramcontent.com/pod-product-compliance
Lightning Source LLC
Chambersburg PA
CBHW051323120626
46547CB00015B/2367